Turn Over Any Stone

Turn Over
Any Stone

Edna Hong

1817

Harper & Row, Publishers, San Francisco

New York, Grand Rapids, Philadelphia, St. Louis
London, Singapore, Sydney, Tokyo, Toronto

FIRST HARPER & ROW EDITION PUBLISHED IN 1990.

Library of Congress Cataloging-in-Publication Data

Hong, Edna Hatlestad
    Turn over any stone   /   Edna Hong.
        p.   cm.
    Reprint. Originally published: Minneapolis: Augsburg, 1970.
    ISBN 0–06–064041–3
        1. Suffering—Religious aspects—Christianity. 2. Consolation.
    I. Title.
    BV4909.H64 1989
    231'.8—dc20   89–29711
                                                                       CIP

90 91 92 93 94   FAIR   10 9 8 7 6 5 4 3 2 1

To Judy and Bliss, Bob and Betsy,
and all who are native citizens of Paindom,
where I am but a tourist

Contents

Turn Over Any Stone

The Thirteenth Fairy

"Oh," she said, coming into the kitchen, where I had gone to punch down the bread dough. "I almost don't like to see my baby beside any other baby."

In the swift glint of tears, I read Naomi's sudden fear that time was carrying her toward something she was unprepared to bear but which would come all the same. Her mind swooped and clutched the bat of fear that had darted and dipped into its house for the first time and banished it to a secret solitary cell.

"Your bread is going over!" she laughed. "I remember how you always forgot the bread rising, and how it grew over the edge of the big yellow bowl, and stretched and broke off in hunks, and if a hunk of dough fell on the floor you made a loaf of it and baked it for whatever dog we happened to have at the time. And when the bread was baked, we kids smelled it and came tearing in and sometimes ate the dog's loaf before anyone could warn us."

"It doesn't seem to have harmed you," I said.

"It was, is, and ever shall be the best bread in the world," she said.

Naomi went back to the living room, where the two newest granddaughters, born three months ago and thousands of miles apart, lay side by side on the same blanket for the first time. And the difference between them was not simply and solely that one was fair of skin and blonde of hair and the other had thrush-brown skin and hair and lashes of soft, lustrous black.

Plucking at the straying tatters of dough and folding them back into the bowl, I somehow knew that Nani, my beautiful Hawaiian grandchild with the dark, inscrutable, unlaughing eyes, concealed a mystery.

I knew that Naomi, my youngest daughter, a stranger to the taste of grief, was soon to give birth all over again—this time to pain—and her pain was already gathering within my breast.

Nani, Nani, my pretty one, are you bitter fruit? A garbled and diminished self? Did nature rudely abandon you before you were finished and go on to something else? Are you bewitched from your mother's womb? Was there a sullen thirteenth fairy who, even before your mother bore you for a long and happy life, came with a cackling, crackling laugh and wished you ill—a future full of ill? Did her evil wand touch the classical geometry of genes that is an infant's body-birthright and disorder it?

That tiny thumb set askew, as if a worker at the assembly belt in the womb factory fell asleep momentarily and blundered—does it mean other and hidden flaws?

You *do* see, we know, for your ebony eyes follow the movements of life but make no comment—no comment whatever on life.

Your little cousin is already decoding her environment, translating it into meaning. Her merry blue eyes expound her critique. Deep in her throat she advances her thesis and propounds that life is good and life is love.

But you, Nani, I search your eyes in vain for your deductions and inferences and find enigma. It seems to make no difference if we stay, or go, or come back. Life seems to be neither wondrous nor dull to you. Does nothing mean anything? Does everything mean nothing?

Do you hear? Do your father's deep-toned, full-voweled Hawaiian lullabies, his softly strumming ukulele, find a clear but winding path to your brain?

You cry—far too much, your body tense and rigid, and cannot be comforted. Is this your commentary on life?

Nani, Nani, born of love, born to love, laved in love, will the dim land of your consciousness ever brighten to the waves of love that caress its shores?

Eden Is Burning

When I went to bed that night, my pillow-case was rude, the sheets were harsh, and there was no graciousness in the April moon. Bats fly at night, and the bats of fear likewise. Mine swooped in and out, dipped up and down, kept sleep a far sigh away.

If my worst fears were true, then why did this have to happen to Naomi, our most vulnerable one—this tender girl who had played with dolls longer than the other ones, who had cut up all our Sears and Montgomery Ward catalogues and created for herself teeming families of unblemished infants and flawless tots—an impeccable progeny, American-dream families, complete with handsome, virile, crewcut fathers and Ford station wagons. Why could Fate not leave this one's little joys alone?

"I want to bring my baby home for the first time in April," she had written. "I want to be in Minnesota in April."

April—but spring is ailing and Eden is burning. The newborn leaf is seared and crimped, forever dead to green, forever dead to life.

About midnight Naomi came into the bedroom quietly and lay in her absent father's place. How I wished that he were not away at this time!

"Mom, do you think that my baby is all right?"

"I think she is beautiful!"

"But *all right,* Mom?"

"What do you mean?" (How my self hated my mind for taking to evasive flight when faced with the unthinkable!)

"I thought she was all right until today when Martha came with her baby, and they're so different! And they shouldn't be, for they were born the same week. My baby doesn't smile, reach out and touch things, coo, gurgle—or anything! She doesn't respond at all!"

Naomi began to cry, but she wept like a beginner to grief. Hers was the dazed, bewildered, puzzled lamentation of one whose joy has fled temporarily, like the sun in a blue sky sliding under a random dark cloud.

And I, the mother who gave her birth, I, who knew that Naomi's world was beginning to unravel, tried to knit it together with a lie.

"But no two babies are ever the same! Any

pediatrician will tell you that an infant never develops just like another one!"

Consoled by my lie, Naomi went back to her room and left me with my birds, dipping wing-wind close. But now fists of self-torment rose out of the batwind and struck at me.

Why, oh, why, are we so often helpless when dear ones cry for help? Why do we falter and fail and leave them in the lurch just then, just when the situation cries out: "Here is the come-at-able, get-at-able, reachable moment. The door is ajar, the way is unclogged. Be true! Be true!"

I lay with closed eyes, but the flames of Naomi's burning Eden flickered on the screen of my eyelids. Quench, quench the fire! Where was the water to quench that fire? A bucket brigade of scraps of Bible verses marched through my mind.

He hath torn, and he will heal. . . .
Cast all your cares. . . .
The oil of joy for mourning. . .
The garment of praise for the spirit of heaviness. . . .

But they were no water, only the dust of empty promises. Indeed, casting them on the fire seemed to make the flames spit and spurt higher.

Words with the weight of authority and the ring of command trooped into my mind:

Is there any one among you suffering?
Let him pray.

Obediently I tried to pray, but all that came was a clutter of agitated words and phrases, all of them beseeching healing for Nani, help for Naomi: "For the sake of Nani, for the sake of Naomi, God, please help! Please help!"

Not until the drab of a relapsed-to-winter dawn did I realize that it was my own Eden—not Naomi's—that was burning. My own insouciant and secure but false paradise was being cremated, and the fuel of the flame constituted "the precious words of comfort," "the sacred words of consolation" I had accumulated in my lifetime in the Church. But the promissory notes were not being paid on demand!

Were they false? Was the deity I was addressing a paper God, as powerless as a fairy godmother? Suddenly I felt as silly as the Old Woman standing frustrated and helpless with the pig that refused to go over the stile, and crying:

> Rope, rope, hang butcher
> Butcher, butcher, kill ox
> Ox, ox, drink water,
> Water, water, quench fire
> Fire, fire burn stick
> Stick, stick, beat dog
> Dog, dog, bite pig
>
> Pig won't go over the stile
> and I won't get home tonight.

Could I, would I, ever go home again to that paradise of pious promises?

And Heaven Is Stone-Deaf

Until the first of May, when Naomi flew with her baby back to the island paradise that was now her home, she and I separately and secretly searched for signs that whispered hope. Alone with Nani, I rallied and distilled all my natural resources of tenderness and love, and sought in vain for a funnel hole through which to pour this quintessence into her opacity.

I even played the clown in trying to evoke a flicker smile. Indeed, I even impersonated a character I despise—the babbling, gushing, cooing, clucking, chin-chucking magpie-grandma—but to no avail. There was no open sesame. My natural, bred-in-the-bone hope snapped and broke.

But Naomi's native, ingrained hope, a greener stick than mine, drank the sap of youth and tilted upward again, especially when Martha left with her baby, and like and unlike no longer cruelly confronted each other. Naomi flew home on the wings of the instinctive optimism of the very young. All is ill and very ill, but all will be well again. Time will heal, time will mend. All will be well again!

In the very young, hope is yeast and hope is east, a habit like the rising sun. But Naomi was flying west in more ways than one, and I trembled to think of the sunset of her immediate, spontaneous hope.

"We're going to take Nani to the best specialist in Hawaii," were her parting words.

The medical reports Naomi included in her letters over the next two years were progressively worse.

"Nani is in a cast. The doctor found that she has something congenitally wrong with her hip."

"The doctor is testing her hearing. There seems to be something wrong with it. Maybe that's why she doesn't respond. But don't worry, Mom and Dad, a lot can be done with a deaf child."

When the seizures began, Naomi panicked and made frequent calls. "They're awful," she sobbed from halfway around the world. "I can't stand to watch her have them."

The seizures were controlled by medication, and the testing went on. The final report also came in a telephone call, in a dull dead voice: "The doctors say that Nani had severe brain damage before birth. She is deaf and untrainable. She probably will never have the mentality of more than a three-month-old baby. The doctor thinks that she should be put in an institution. A place like Barrington, Mom! Barrington!"

The receiver crackled with her wild weeping, and this was the weeping of one who had begun at the beginning and had come a long way into grief.

After a long time: "Mom, are you still there?"

"Yes, oh yes! I'm crying with you!"

"What shall we do? What shall we do?"

You hope and hope and hope and then you do not hope anymore. Hope goes out. All hope goes out, and you do not hope anymore.

Nani, Nani, my pretty one! Every test has subtracted from you. Almost everything human has been taken from you—hearing, talking, walking, feeling, discovering, learning. What remains? Nothing but just being—just subsisting? What kind of subsisting being, Nani, are you?

Seeking an answer to my question, I drove to Barrington and wandered about among the sights, sounds, and smells of a state institution.

The severely retarded, the physically and mentally abnormal—all these defective specimens of humanity who gibber meaninglessly, slobber incessantly, rock monotonously, grab, and gesticulate senselessly or just lie inertly, who often stink in spite of frequent washing and whom we shut away and out of our sight.

On the way home and all that night, I turned my despair and rage upon the Creator. I taunted him. I threw my beautiful blighted grandchild and the whole menagerie of grimacing deformities and monstrosities into his face.

What are you—Creator or Father? If Creator, are *they* your image? Do *you*, then, have a monster head? Are *you* hunchbacked, clubfooted? Do we worship a Divine Freak? Do we pray to a Divine Absurdity, a Supernatural Monster?

If Father, then what happened to all the fatherly virtues: tenderness, protectiveness, affection, solicitude?

Answer me, you who claim to be both Creator and Father. Answer!

But all I got was silence. I scolded him like a shrew. I displayed the temper of a female fiend. I insulted him. I poured out obscenities I did not know I had within me.

But he was silent, and I remembered a verse in a psalm and found it: *Is he deaf, the God who planted the ear?*

No Balms or Bromides

And if I, thousands of space miles removed from the source of pain, I who could never know or feel the fullness of pain that Nani fountained, if *I* was hurling my rage and despair at the Divine Tormentor, what must Nani's parents have been doing, saying, thinking? Were they who leaned over the crib of their perennial infant praying the ageless petition:

Remove thy stroke from me;
I am spent by the blows of thy hand?

Were they piteously pleading for a "Take up thy bed and walk" miracle? Were they comparing their misfortunate selves with the fortunate?

For they have no pangs;
their bodies are sound and sleek.
For they are not in trouble as other men are;
they are not stricken like other men.

Were they hurling eternal, agonized "Why?" at heaven? Why did you do it? Why did you give our baby life and then take away everything that makes life worth living? Explain yourself! Justify yourself!

Where had I read it? Was it Edna St. Vincent Millay?

"Distressed mind,
Forbear to tease the hooded why.
The shape will not reply."

Were Nani's parents, too, meeting only a vast silence? And was it the silence of a cosmic, infinite embarrassment?

Why are you silent, Creator God? Are you in such a pickle, you who keep your rod in pickle, that you cannot answer? Would you rather not own up to being the Author of such an inhuman mess as the human mess you have created? We are not complaining of our man-made mess but of yours: the maiming and the paining of the innocents. And if you did not create the sufferings of the innocent, why do you consent to all that happens, and how?

And you, Savior, Mediator, Intercessor, the Lamb of God, the Man of Sorrows, Son of God and Son of Man, why are *you* silent? Have you forgotten what it means to be human, the giant agony of being human, and therefore you are silent? Or are you silent because you remember so well?

And you, the most neglected member of the Trinity, you, the Holy Spirit, the Dove, the Comforter, the Consoler, the Counselor—why are *you* silent?

Has the job of consoling the unconsolable become so depressing and so dis-spiriting that you have closed your practice?

O Divine Indifference, we cry out for sounds that mean something. Words, real words, authentic words! Not the pat, fat phrases of the mealy-mouthed pious, not "devotional helps," "lessons for life learned from life," "peace of mind" platitudes. (Those whose pain has no exit are forever exiled from "peace of mind"!)

Words, real words! Not new scientific psychological dogmas (by now we know that newness does not spell success, and the patients get no better).

Words, real words! Not the existentialists' counsel of brave despair: "Life is ultimate tragedy, ha, ha! But have the courage to be." (How does one *get* that courage to be?)

Where were the words to come from when no springs spurted from God's unspeakingness, science's helplessness, the intellectuals' hopelessness? We might as well talk to a rock about our grief!

Yet there had to be real words. Youthful optimism had toppled, buoyant spontaneous hope had had its deathblow, and I knew, I knew in the innermost depths of my being the exhaustion, the paralysis, the despair in the wake of such a loss.

But I also knew now as never before that the words could not come from me. I had no answers. No tranquilizers for mental distress on my shelves. No tonics for despondency. No antidotes for the poison of suffering. No wealth of wisdom for the bankruptcy of spontaneous, immediate hope. No clues to the paindom!

If we, Naomi's parents, could not say anything to alter our daughter's anguish over her firstborn, could we perhaps *do* something?

"Should *you* go to her or should I?" I asked her father. "Or should we bring her and the baby home for a time?"

Something within us said, "No." In those very hours and days and weeks when we were most anxious and concerned about Naomi, when we yearned to take her in our arms and speak to her pain all the tender, compassionate, loving words we knew, something told us to keep the distance of an ocean between us.

And this is how I began to realize that God is perhaps more concerned when he is silent, when he seems to have stepped aside or withdrawn, than at any other time!

This is how I began to discern, to my bitter shame, the unworthiness and the obtuseness of calling divine silence the death of God—to say nothing of my browbeating God! I had not mocked God; I had mocked myself. I had not harmed God. I had harmed myself.

In such a mood, I discovered words, real words, words so real that they came with the effect of a bomb rather than of a bromide. Strangely enough, Psalm 73 addressed itself to *me* and not to Naomi!

When my soul was embittered,
when I was pricked in heart,
I was stupid and ignorant,
I was like a beast toward thee.
Nevertheless I am continually with thee;
thou dost hold my right hand.
Whom have I in heaven but thee?
My flesh and my heart may fail,
but God is the strength of my heart
and my portion forever.

Is There a Formula for Suffering?

For two years Nani's parents shifted between two poles: joy and pain.

Joy with its hope of the possible. Perhaps. Maybe. There may be a chance. It is possible. God willing.

Pain with its consciousness of the impossible. No hope at all. No chance whatsoever. It is hopeless. It is impossible. God is not willing.

Gradually the burden of proof and the weight of evidence shifted to the pain pole. The unthinkable was not only thinkable, it was undeniable, unmistakable. There was no hope.

Shortly before the scales tipped irrevocably to the impossible, Naomi wrote a letter that indicated that she was fully aware that this was coming. It was stream-of-consciousness writing—the consciousness rushing down mind-mountains and mind-cliffs to the ocean of inevitability.

"We want to keep Nani so much—oh, we love her more and more—we don't know what will happen—it's strange—I've never really had the thought before—I know it's useless upsetting ourselves—but what will happen to Nani when she is as old as we are now? She is so beautiful and healthy—but completely helpless. I think it's our hopes that hurt the most—or maybe the fears—I can't imagine what it is like to be her—can she think? We don't know what to do—oh, I can't do it! Oh, I know I can! I don't think like this all the time. It kills me when I do!"

It was the last sentence that chilled me: "I don't think like this all the time. It kills me when I do."

Naomi cannot, she must not, be "killed." It was not the fear of physical death that haunted me, because Naomi had demonstrated several times that her life instinct was imperious. It was the suffocating and the killing of her spirit that I feared, the slow strangling when a stone, an irreducible something, is planted in the soul, and the spirit can no longer breathe freely and deeply. The breath of the spirit becomes more and more shallow—until there is no perceptible breath, and the spirit is as if dead.

Pain resisted could be this killer, this stone. It could be even more; it could be a foreign malignant body that not only lies there in the soul inert and irreducible but also exudes the suffocating carbon dioxide of despondency, defiance, and despair.

Pain resisted could intensify, worsen the pain. Any woman who has given birth knows the consequences of stiffening her body against the contractions of the uterus in its uncompromising will to deliver its freight. Birth pangs resisted give no quarter, become ruthless and relentless. If the body's resistance is as relentless and ruthless as the uterus's determination to give birth, the body may have to submit to Caesarean incision. If it will not assent to the pain of birth, it will have to assent to a wound.

But in and of itself pain is a wound; indeed, all creation seems to bear the wound of pain. As the old adage goes, "Man is born in another's pain and perishes in his own." Pain lies at the center of existence in the same way as Nani is the nucleus of pain in her parents' daily life.

The mystery of Nani! Would it be necessary to go through the dark valley of Nani to find the mystery of pain and suffering? And if all of us who loved Nani did not learn the mystery, were we doomed to learn bitterness, tension, depression, resentment, meaninglessness?

Do suffering and pain have a formula?

And the solution to suffering, too?

Suffering $= a^2 + 3ab + b^4$?

Solution to Suffering $= x^5 - 3(x-2y) - 4y^2$?

If I could master the mathematics of pain, if I could learn the alphabet of suffering, could I, if necessary, help my daughter to creep again, to walk again, or even to fly again—in the spirit?

But how can one work out equations (or a gospel) for suffering when there are so few givens, and the givens are all negative? And were they really givens, or my personal, private intuitions, based mainly on fear that Naomi, who had stumbled into a path of suffering, unchosen and inescapable, would in time reach the limit of her endurance and would travel some descending path?

My only positive intuition—certainly not a given—was that suffering is cloaked in mystery and yet has a mystery to reveal. If Naomi did not learn this mystery, her spirit might be killed. Could I, her mother, unravel the mystery? Could I find a daybreak that could become another's dawning?

No Ancient Solution

They could have been contemporaries—the Greek poet Homer, the Hebrew poet David, and the unknown Hebrew who met the problem of the suffering of the innocent head-on in the Book of Job.

Enticed by the glamor of the less familiar, I steered my quest for a solution to suffering first to the Greek pagan mind. The year 1000 B.C. was a different age from ours, but I soon discovered that the essential problem of living was the same, its pain was the same, and its tears were the same.

In the first and greatest of antiquity's pagan poets I heard the universal lament of the bereaved mother in the cry of Hector's mother: "My child, ah, woe is me! Wherefore should I live in my pain, Now that thou art dead . . . ?"

The world of man was very young in 1000 B.C., but the shadow of impending catastrophe hung over life even then. Achilles said as much to the father of the dead Hector: "This is the lot the gods have spun for miserable men, that they should live in pain, yet themselves are without sorrow."

"Reckon no man happy," said Creon in *Oedipus the King,* "until you witness the closing day, until he passes the border which severs life from death, unscathed by sorrow."

The ancient Greeks knew the existential fact of human suffering. But a solution to suffering?

I read the epics, the tragedies, the comedies (which were never far from tears), but I found no equations. Helpless victims of fate are defenseless and formulate no formulas. Nevertheless—and the glory of Homer and of the Greeks is in that one word *nevertheless*—they accepted life as a glorious adventure and lived it so. Face to face with the mystery of death, often sudden and violent death, they lived the mystery of joyous life. They seemed to find goodness even in the taste of the salt of tears!

As I read on in ancient Greek literature, I saw the dawn of the idea that the seeds of self-destruction, of pain and suffering, are in the interior being. By the time the great Greek tragedians began writing (500–400 B.C.) the Greeks had developed the concept of *hubris,* the sin of pride, that human beings by their own insolence and impudence can call down the punitive wrath of the gods, and thus be responsible for capsizing their own ship of life. But not even Socrates understood that the dark passions that create havoc and suffering on the human scene are so deeply ingrained that they cannot be eradicated by knowledge, by sweetness and light! Not even you, Socrates, noblest of the pagans, had a radical solution!

Still bypassing the Hebrew desert poets, David, and the poet of Job, I searched the pagan mind farther and farther to the East. Admittedly I scratched only the surface of literature, but wherever I scratched I found an underlying human scene as modern as today. I found the earth saturated with human tears, "soaked from its crust to its core," as Ivan said in *The Brothers Karamazov.*

Often I found the dim dawning of the idea that the human personality is a paradoxical thing for which no formula can be found. In the Persian epic *Firdausi,* Rustem, the unwitting slayer of his own son, Sohrab, saw himself as the "spring of all this scene of woe." Some few of the ancient pagan minds perceived that there is nothing fixed and tangible either in one's mind or nature, that lends itself to a human equation that will solve one's own dilemma.

In the literature of the Far East, however, I found very conscious efforts to create a formula for suffering. Indeed, the religions of the Far East were structured as simple equations: Solution to Suffering = Indifference.

Indifference to pleasure as well as to pain. Indifference to gain as well as to loss, to victory as well as to defeat. Desire nothing for oneself, for all that the senses desire is nothing.

But in and of itself the solution, the equation, the religion was a shrinking in pain from the spectacle of human pain! This was no solution at all, since it created an even greater paradox in the human personality and engaged individuals in an utterly self-centered and selfish striving to be selfless.

The mind of the Far East may still cry:"I know the answer to pain. I have found it. It is to be indifferent." But its painfully cultivated indifference is nothing more than a shriek of pain, muffled and stifled! Its claim to a solution merely affirms its solidarity with all human suffering!

Ancient Wisdom,
But No Formulas

With dragging feet, like an adolescent finally but reluctantly turning to old parents to find the wisdom she has hopefully and vainly sought elsewhere, I turned to the Old Testament.

I came prepared to find suffering but not to discover that the entire Old Testament is an epic of a suffering nation, that in some ways the name "Israel" is synonymous with suffering. I was prepared to find circumstances of particular suffering.

David's heartrending cry at the death of his traitor son will always ring in my ears:

O my son Absalom,
My son, my son Absalom!
Would I had died instead of you,
O Absalom, my son, my son!

But I was not prepared to find again and again the figure of the Suffering Servant who takes upon himself the full weight of ephemeral and afflicted human life.

I was prepared for pious platitudes and practical prudence on the subject of suffering, and the Proverbs for the most part bore out my expectations:

The fear of the Lord prolongs life
but the years of the wicked will be short.

The righteous is delivered from trouble
and the wicked gets into it instead.

No ill befalls the righteous,
but the wicked are filled with trouble.

I was even prepared for the psalmists' bewilderment and resentment that their simple equations did not seem to work out in actuality. Righteousness did not always equal success, prosperity, felicity, and bliss. Unrighteousness did not always equal failure, adversity, sorrow, and tribulation. I was prepared to hear the psalmists cry out, "It isn't fair! It isn't fair!" and so they did.

But I was totally unprepared for the fury of the Hebrews' anger against wickedness and for the depth of their own grief and penitence when they found themselves to be guilty of wickedness.

In the pagan literature I had found lasciviousness and cold cruelties pretty much taken for granted, but not here in the Old Testament! Here the righteous almost seemed to luxuriate in their hatred of unrighteousness. Was the pagan tolerance due to their belief in gods who were themselves lascivious and prone to fits of petulant cruelty? Did the Hebrew hatred of sin flow from their God, who was implacably hostile to sin but at the same time utterly concerned for the sinner? So concerned, in fact, that he seemed to have his own private hell of pain and suffering, and it was his love for his human children!

He cared enough for them to place within them an infinite goal of perfection, to stand in judgment upon their failure to strive toward that goal, to discipline and punish them for rebelling against that infinite goal. Yet all the time he was acting in his fatherly role of "bringing up the children," he experienced a father's agony at seeing his children go astray and writhe in their own self-made torments.

Truly there was no god like this God, the God of the Hebrews, this God who was at one with his children despite their rebellion, despite their affliction! It was almost as if I, a spiritual adolescent, had to see and scrutinize other parents, other gods, before I realized the superiority of my own parent, my own God!

But still not a word to unravel the riddle of suffering! Still no clues to Nani! I had found various modes of living in the face of suffering. The Greek pagan walked boldly on the thin thread of life the Fates spun and, if it was cut, was hurled into the abyss and fell without whimpering. The Eastern pagan contemplated away pain as well as pleasure and dreamed of a better reincarnation and the ultimate bliss of perfect peace. He looked forward to the end of a life of self-conscious being and absorption into the Absolute. As for the Hebrews, whatever their suffering condition—as slaves, deportees, or refugees (and they were almost always one of these!)—they *exulted* in their God. They exulted even in their God's severe Law and in their God's constant searching out the secret depths of the human soul.

It took centuries of cudgeling to hammer into the Hebrew skull the idea that pleasure and prosperity are *not* God's reward for righteousness, nor are pain and affliction his punishment for unrighteousness.

The Book of Job, that most splendid creation of Hebrew poetry, toppled that naive notion once and for all in its message that God is a transcendent God whose ways are beyond finding out and whose purposes are inscrutable. God is God, and he is to be served for love and not for reward. Yes, one *exults in God* in the midst of deepest affliction of body, mind, and spirit—in deepest despair.

Job had to descend to the lowest depths of despair to explode the rosy moral equation that identified happiness and prosperity with righteousness and God's reward, and pain and tribulation with God's punishment. His mind almost departed from sanity when he contemplated how

from out of the city the dying groan,
and the soul of the wounded cries for help,
yet God pays no attention to their prayer.

But when Job's friends continued to cling to their narrow view of suffering, his mind broke through to a new view of suffering and of the human being's relationship to God. If Job had sung a psalm after his breakthrough, he would have sung:

Praise the Lord!
Praise the Lord, O my soul!
Praise him in loss.
Praise him in anguish.
Praise him in pain.
I will praise the Lord in every condition.
I will sing praises to the Lord as long as I live.
I will sing praises to my God while I have being.

And Job's psalm would have had a newness that the psalms ascribed to David did not have.

But could Naomi sing this new psalm? On the strength of Job's new wisdom, could she sing her own psalm:

Praise the Lord. Praise him for Nani. Praise him for her damaged brain. Praise him for her seizures. Praise him for her deaf muteness. The Lord is just in all his ways. The Lord is kind in all his doings.

Poet of Job, you were wise, the wisest of all the wisdom poets. But suffering is still a paradox, still the darkest and strangest of life's paradoxes. And what comfort and consolation is there in a paradox?

But These Little Ones!

Leaving the Old Testament writers, I stood at the door of the New Testament but did not go in. This time my reluctance was something deeper than spiritual adolescence.

My mind told me it was because the New Testament was all about personal salvation and therefore could not and would not illuminate the problem of pain and suffering, that it would supply no meaning for Nani, no comfort for Naomi.

My heart told me that my notion was a pettifogging lie and that my mind was evading and avoiding the real reason for stalling at the door of the New Testament, because the real reason would be incriminating.

My mind scoffed at the very idea. How could a sincere, honest, old grandmother diligently searching for a meaning for her brain-damaged grandchild possibly be incriminated?

But I did not go in. I am ashamed to say that I not only leaped over the New Testament, but over centuries of Christian literature, including that of Augustine, Dante, and John Bunyan.

My mind sprinted as fast as it could to one whom it had met years before and dimly remembered as having wrestled with the enigma of innocent suffering—namely, Ivan in *The Brothers Karamazov.* Ivan was tormented by the same doubt that tormented Job and was tormenting me. How can one believe that a God who allows even one innocent child to suffer is a just God?

But where Job's faith floundered on his own undeserved afflictions, Ivan's faith and my own floundered on the sufferings of children. Less sure of our own innocence, more doubtful of our own righteousness before God, and more aware than Job of the odious, vicious, and diabolical self that coexists in our beings, we could not take Job's self-righteous stance. But we stood on sure ground for rebellion when it came to the sufferings of children! For me, Nani was reason enough to challenge a God who gives a life but withholds everything that makes life worth living.

"'I say nothing of the sufferings of grown-up people,' said Ivan to Alyosha, 'they have eaten the apple, damn them, and the devil take them all. . . . But these little ones? . . . If all must suffer to pay for the eternal harmony, what have children to do with it? And if it is really true that they must share responsibility for the father's crimes, such a truth is not of this world and is beyond my comprehension. . . . I want to see with my own eyes the hind lie down with the lion and the victim rise up and embrace his murderer. I want to be there when every one suddenly understands what it has all been for. All the religions of the world are built on this longing, and I am a believer. But then there are the children, and what am I to do about them? That's a question I can't answer. For the hundredth time I repeat, there are numbers of questions, but I've only taken the children, because in their case what I mean is so unanswerably clear. . . . If the sufferings of children go to swell the sum of sufferings which was necessary to pay for truth, then I protest that the truth is not worth such a price. . . . And so I hasten to give back my entrance ticket. . . . It's not God that I don't accept, Alyosha, only I must respectfully return Him the ticket.'"

Had he not "handed in his ticket," Ivan would have been a nineteenth-century Job. By handing in his ticket, he retained his intellectual integrity—and lost his faith.

And I? If I found no illumination, no meaning, no equation for suffering, the sufferings of the innocent, would I, too, eventually hurl my entrance ticket to the eternal harmony of eternity, where there is no more suffering? Would I hurl it into the face of the Supernatural Monster who, if he did not contrive it, nevertheless *allowed* the existence of this mortal disharmony?

Another Russian, Belinsky, once said that "harmony itself is conditioned by disharmony. This may be gratifying for lovers of music, but it certainly is not for those who are doomed to express disharmony in their own experience."

After reading and rereading Ivan's brilliant and profound treatment of Job's question, I was suddenly alarmed to discover that the quest for a meaning for suffering to give my daughter was taking a painful turn. I had set my plowshare in the soil of the world's great literature and turned up human pain and human grieving, but I was also turning up something else that I did not wish to turn up. The plowshare had turned inward and was disturbing ground that I did not wish disturbed.

Some Cold Computations

W as it to prevent the uncovering of humiliating contradictions within my own self that I suddenly decided to stop looking in literature for the *meaning* of pain and suffering and looked instead for *reactions* to pain and suffering? Was it because I sensed the danger of getting into something with all my being that I stopped looking for something about which I could say: "Now I know it! I have found it!" Was the cold objectifying method of my next search and summary of reactions to pain a frightened retreat from subjectivity?

Whatever the reason, here are the somewhat chilly, compassionless conclusions I drew up after reading, night after night, this modern literature that seems to have no god against whom it can hurl its "why." (Hence writers today are often not much more than uninhibited and unembarrassed gossipers of despair, purveyors of the miseries and misfortunes of the human race. Strangely enough, the psychic suffering of fictional human beings in literature seemed to become more terrible when they stopped asking "why" and began to regard pain and suffering as utterly meaningless!)

But here is my outline of human reactions to pain in modern literature:

I. Evasion

A fugitive from pain, the "evader" steers his life around all stresses and distresses, keeps anguish at a distance, out of hearing. By averting his eyes and holding his nose, by plugging his ears and shunning all entangling alliances, he manages to avoid every suggestion of the tragic and develops the callous hide of a rhinoceros. By pursuing pleasures rapaciously (sensually, esthetically, and intellectually—according to his temperament and gentility) he does indeed evade the agonies of pain by day, but his nights are stitched with pain and preyed upon by bloodless shapes as pale and inhuman as his own self.

II. Dilution

Time dilutes any pain that has an ending, but the "diluter" hastens the watering-down process with bracers, pills, and pick-me-ups and countless clever compensations. She manufactures a silly, sleazy optimism, flabby and soporific, that mitigates the pain—or seems to. Or she dilutes her pain by spreading it. She pouts and piques and knifes and wounds. Every good and beautiful thing is a personal insult, and she must smear it with her bitter bile.

Or she creates a compensatory Kingdom of God, an artificial paradise, the best of all possible artificial paradises, where God-on-a-leash dispenses success and happiness to those he favors, failure and wretchedness to those he disfavors, and consecrates every pain-palliative. Determined to be happy, the "diluter" dilutes her suffering with a mediocrity that God finds insufferable!

III. Submersion

The "submerger" embraces his suffering, takes it to bed with him at night, fondles and feels and caresses it as if it were his favorite mistress. The "submerger" gormandizes his afflictions, tastes his pain and savors its unsavoriness, smells the fragrance of its foulness. The "submerger" listens to the throbbing of his anguished heart, takes the temperature of his misery hourly, measures his pain pressure, and thrives on all the symptoms of his ills and griefs.

I still don't know why I attempted to catalog and computerize human reactions to pain and suffering in modern literature: all the way from the total collapse of "I cannot endure it!" to the jutting-jaw, self-willed tenacity of "By God, I will endure it!" I can only explain it now as the dodge of sophistry, the dishonesty of speculating about something that one is beginning to experience too painfully and keenly.

All the time I was savagely computerizing inadequate reactions to human suffering, I myself was guilty of one of the most common of inadequate reactions and compensations! Was it perhaps significant that the dodge of sophistry about suffering did not appear in my catalogue?

Overthrowing the Dictator

Then, within the space of twenty-four hours, two things happened that were totally unexpected and implicit nudges to do something I had not even remotely considered. Omitting all the "whens," "wheres," and "whys," I need only say that I encountered a woman I had never seen before and perhaps may never see again. The encounter lasted but five minutes.

"At the countdown of four," I told my Partner, "we had taken care of the amenities. By three we were conversing in depth. At one she gave me a copy of Herman Hesse's *Siddhartha*, and at zero she rocketed off, and our orbits will probably never cross again."

In reading the book that night, I was absorbed not by Siddhartha's lifelong quest for truth but by the *river*, the river to which Siddhartha went, wounded and disillusioned by life, the river where he learned to know love and serenity. Siddhartha loved a river the way our family loves a river in the wilderness of forest along the Canadian border. The strange woman with whom I had spoken but five minutes had given me a book about a seeker who loved a river and listened to it, listened "with a still heart and a waiting, open soul, without passion, without desire, without judgment, without opinions."

The next day's mail brought a new poem from Bob, a friend who is a native citizen of the Kingdom of Pain. He was writing what he whimsically called psongs, twelve-line poems based on the psalms. This one had flowed out of Psalm 42:

> As a deer thirsts for running streams,
>   so my soul longs for You, O God.
>   My tears have been my only food;
> men taunt me with 'Where is your God?'
>   God, my soul is in agony.
>   Ocean deeps call to ocean deeps
>   in the roar of Your waterfall.
>   All of Your waves break in my soul!
>   Why are you in despair, my soul,
>   Why do you know such turbulence?
>   Wait for God! Hope expectantly,
>   for I shall yet praise Him for help!

Again it was not the despairing soul, the soul in agony, that dispossessed all other thoughts, but the "running streams," the "roar of your waterfall."

And the "Wait for God! Hope expectantly, for I shall yet praise Him for help!"

The strange coincidence of the gift of the book and the poem ... all in the same day, created an overwhelming longing for our northwoods river, and the feeling quickly became a compulsion, a necessity, an urgency. The nudging had become so strong that I actually felt rib-sore, just as one feels tension in knotted stomach muscles and fear in cold, goose-fleshed skin.

My Partner, who understands me better, I sometimes feel, than I do myself, let me go by myself immediately to be alone with the river.

Siddhartha came to his river with the wound of a meaningless life. I came to my river with the wound of a beloved child's meaningless suffering. Siddhartha lived out his lifetime on his river and found his truth. I hoped to find my meaning on my river in the single month of June.

It was this sense of urgent expectancy that nearly frustrated the whole effort.

In the first place, I saw Naomi everywhere on the river, which she loves as much as I do. I could see her swimming across the rapids to the huge, safe boulders on the other side for the first time—her eyes wide and wild with an admixture of fear, hope, trust, and joy.

I could see her draped on one of the huge, sun-warmed boulders in the middle of the river, reading happy-ending novels and weeping quietly when one happened not to end that way. Over the years the boulders had acquired names: The Chair, The Couch, The Table, The Throne, The Saddle, The Giantess Lap, Gog and Magog, and each time I passed them, I saw her slim, tanned body molded to one or another.

In the second place, whether I was in or on the river, my mind kept making metaphors and creating parables out of every sight, sound, and sensation I experienced. For example, the mosquitoes and migs in the northwoods in June are wicked demolishers of contemplation, but a spraying of insect repellent held them a few comfortable insect-lengths away.

"Aha!" said my adumbrating mind. "We humans hold off pain and suffering just like that. A throb of pain—take an aspirin. A droning of depression—take a tranquillizer. A hint of tiredness—take a pep pill."

When, after lying prone on The Table boulder for an hour, watching the skater bugs glide fluently among the foam bubbles in the amber water, I discovered that the skater bugs cast a shadow of four balanced plump dots around a center—and that foam bubbles cast hardly a shadow, my hound dog mind bayed excitedly.

I have a little shadow
that goes in and out with me
and what can be the use of him
is more than I can see.

Pain is everyone's shadow—and only things with substance cast a shadow. Nonentities are not vested with shadow. Can pain, then, be meaningless? Hollow men do not suffer as much pain as whole men. Do hollow men cast a shadow?

When my feet rediscovered the hidden but safe bracing rocks at the foot of the waterfall, and I leaned into the surging, buffeting, battering cascade until my reddened body was dissenting but exhilarated, once again my mind went to work turning this too into grist for its gist-mill.

The fussy little dictator on his bone-throne in my cranium did not surrender until I spent my entire day totally concentrated, physically and mentally, on making a path along the river to an otherwise inaccessible beautiful gorge and waterfall. That night I fell into bed exhausted, slept a dreamless sleep, and woke to a mind that was no longer conceiving parables for its own gospel, nor dictating its own answers.

Stopped at the Border

The next day June reverted to April's cloudiness and coolness. On any other day I would have stoked the wood range with big chunks of birch, built a fire in the fireplace, and read all day in cabin comfort, but reading would only make my mind talkative again. Our family had already discovered that on such a day swimming in the river is not only tolerable but utterly pleasurable if wedded to a sauna.

So I had my day on the river anyway, alternately roasting in tropical heat on the top shelf of the sauna and swimming in the frigid water of the river. The warmth lingered long in the sauna after the fire subsided, and I lay on my stomach looking out the window at the river foaming and cascading through the deep cleft it had made in the black basalt rock through millions of spring torrents. Or I closed my eyes and listened to the sound that anywhere else but here would have terrified me, for it was not unlike the roaring when a violent midwestern storm breaks the dull, stupid torpor of a hot and humid summer day. Here on the river the sound was pure Beethoven.

I fell asleep sauna-warm and naked, and awoke chilled and feeling that the afternoon was fast sliding toward night.

It was not until I had climbed the cliff path to the cabin and the tea kettle was singing and the coffee pot perking that I was aware that something had happened. I had floated free from a distorted and distorting mood and was existentially moving toward a new happening, a new "awaring." My mind had first assaulted heaven with rage and despair over Nani, and then had frantically and frenetically labored to find a meaning that would encompass and explain her suffering and all suffering, voluntary and involuntary. Now my mind had finally been brought to a standstill, and a profound change seemed to be taking place between myself and the mystery of the suffering.

Was this standstill perhaps necessary? Does one have to stand and wait patiently on the border of a new continent of awareness and wait for a visa to enter? Does one have to be stripped and searched there and divested of every perception, preconception, prejudice, and mood that could be alien coin in this new country? Socrates had had to stand still to come to himself.

Gunnar Myrdal in his preface to *Asian Drama* wrote: "When men have learned not to be frustrated because their wishes are not immediately fulfilled and not to be bitter because the world has proved tougher and more complex than they had dreamed, then they may be in a mood to value truth very highly."

My anger, bitterness, and despair had vanished. As yet my truth, my meaning, was imperceptible—not even a hint on the distant mindscape—but the barrier to it was gone.

It was a humbling experience. I realized that what I, with my little sprinkling of adversities, had come slap up against was *not*—as I had thought—the wall of the pain and suffering of my daughter Naomi over her firstborn child, but the wall of my own interior jungle.

My daughter's pain had entered my being and broken its apparently sweet harmony. The dissonance of my jungle, which had always been there in *pianissimo*, had become pandemonium *fortissimo*, and now all was quiet. But not the same quiet as before!

Moreover, the barriers to the new awareness, whatever it would be, were down.

What about Naomi, living at the agonizing center, the pivotal point of pain, and experiencing what I felt only at its edge? Was she also moving out of dazed pandemonium toward a new happening, a new awaring? Had her mind, too, ceased to demand divine apologies and explanations and become silent?

In my own silence there in the cabin, I knew that Naomi's could be another kind of silence. It could be a locking of the grief and pain in the unconscious, a trying-to-be-happy by not thinking about it. But any one-headed creature of our interior jungle we relegate to the silence of the unconsciousness emerges in unexpected places and at unexpected times with two or three heads, and the dissonance is augmented by that many more mouths with which to shriek.

Thus Naomi, brought to a standstill by pain and suffering, and I, her mother, brought to a standstill by her pain and suffering, stood at the border of two continents: one that transcended self-pity, depression, and despair and brought a new relationship to the suffering; and one, a subcontinent, where demons sucked at the grief, fed upon the suffering, and begot a progeny of baleful brats.

The Subcontinent of No

There was little sleep for me that night, for my mind suddenly was released from the request to be silent and carried on a lively dialogue with thoughts that were not my own—at least they came out of the night like virgins with brightly trimmed lights.

For a while as I lay wide awake watching the stars and planets slide across the cabin window that looked down the river, I felt as if these thoughts and I were about to make a landing on this new continent to which the stillness had brought me, but gradually it became clear that it was the subcontinent we were to visit this night, the subcontinent of No, the Land of Negation, inhabited by No-persons who live there by chance or by choice.

If Naomi were to settle down in this gray No-Continent, it would be by chance, by sliding toward it in an ambiguous sort of way when the downweight of existential life proved to be greater than the uplift of her youthful life forces. When the bright expectations of youth went out, one by one, as they inevitably do (and this blackish grief of hers could hasten the inevitability) she *could* find herself an unwilling but permanent resident of this subcontinent. For Naomi, as it has been for countless others, it would be a *descent* from the Kingdom of the First Spontaneity to the gray coasts of Null.

"How does it really happen?" my mind asked its virgin visitors.

The brightest of them answered: "Almost imperceptibly for those who inhabit the Kingdom of the First Spontaneity long past its season. There is enough vital fluid in youthful first spontaneity to take care of the April showers which into each life must fall. And God is good and God is love, and God is in his heaven, and all is right with the world.

"When surprised by large griefs and astonished by sinister afflictions, the young invent fictions to think themselves happy. And God is still good and God is love, and God is in his heaven, and all is right with the world.

"When their buoyant hopes of being beautiful people and living beautiful lives in a beautiful world are grounded, they modify their lives to soften the bitterness. And God is still good and God is love, and God is in his heaven, and all is right with the world.

"They structure their lives to avoid the sights and sounds and smells of suffering and know not true suffering but only the frustration of their attempts to structure their lives to avoid the sights and sounds and smells of suffering. And God is still good and God is still love, and God is still in his heaven, and all is still right with the world.

"They bypass all the possibilities that menace existence—the possibility of unhappiness, the possibility of despair, the possibility of offense—and in the end this proves to be the greatest menace of all and causes their downfalling to the subcontinent of No, for they never learn to their utter astonishment that they are not what they imagine themselves to be. Indeed, they are nothing, their happiness is nothing, their security is nothing, and their God and their heaven are the most fraudulent fiction.

"For never to move out of the Kingdom of the First Spontaneity is to become an involuntary No-person and to descend to the subcontinent of No.

"To fortify this kingdom against the mortal combat between Yes and No in this world, against the pain and suffering of that combat, is to descend to the subcontinent of No. To refuse to join the struggle between the forces of Yes and No in this world, to say No to the struggle, is to descend to the subcontinent of No. In a way they can be said to be April-fooled into the subcontinent, and yet it is not entirely innocent, their descending. Perhaps it is more correct to say that they are not there by choice but by reason of a thousand little choices outly and not inly prompted.

"But some have *elected* this subcontinent of No, have voted No to the Yes, Yes to the No. Confronted with the stark truths of life—Dachau, Lidice, Hiroshima, Vietnam, Nigeria, leukemia, Parkinson's disease, meaninglessness, death ("Man is being-to-ward-death," they say)—they surrender to hopelessness and despair, call existence absurd, and write bitter comedies about it."

"Yes, oh yes!" I interrupted excitedly. "I read something like that in Kierkegaard's *Journals* not long ago and wrote it into my own journal." I lit a candle, found the notebook, and so strong was my feeling of carrying on a dialogue with the virgin thoughts that I read it aloud.

"'All is phony, so let us laugh. Everything is lousy, so let us clink the glasses. . . . ' What an abyss of perdition! At the bottom of it all lies despair. To want to do even the least bit to halt this demoralization . . . this they would regard as ridiculous. 'Let it hit bottom!' And although we sink in it, we entertain ourselves with witty comedies that expose the perdition. 'Done for,' they say. 'We are done for. Nobody should complain about anybody. So let's all laugh—the crazier the better. Let's not only be wretched—let's refine it with cleverness and wit and dramatize it brilliantly.'"

And it was there in the candlelight I found another note of Kierkegaard's I had jotted down several years before and forgotten completely: "The ground and meaning of suffering: dying to immediacy—and that a man achieves nothing—nothing at all by himself—dying to immediacy and remaining in finiteness."

There it was. Dying to the first immediacy. Spiritual bankruptcy. Choose now where you shall dwell: *Either* in the subcontinent of No, *Or* in the continent of Yes!

This, then, is what suffering can and does do. The mind that comes slap up against pain also comes slap up against life's most crucial Either/Or.

The Wound of Grace

Washing clothes at the cabin is an enchant-ing task. I place the copper kettle on the wood range, dipper amber river water into it, cut thick slabs of yellow soap into it, and immerse the soiled clothes. When fragrant steam begins to rise from the kettle, I leave my reading intermittently to poke and turn the clothes with the handle of a long wooden spoon. When the fire has died down and the water cooled to lukewarm, I wring out the clothes and carry them down the cliff path to the river to rinse.

It was while I was sitting on my rinsing rock that next morning, chin in hand, anchoring a sheet against another rock with my bare feet while it bil-lowed down the current and was flushed of suds, that the idea of the "wound of grace" hit me.

Having been brought up on the concept of grace as an oil, an herb, a balm, an unction, the idea of grace as a wound was so astonishing that I instinctively drew up my legs and lost the sheet to the river. But what is one old, worn and mended sheet to a fresh and brand-new concept? The sheet would wrap itself around some boulder far downstream and remain attached there until it disintegrated, whereas my new concept cut my mind loose from an educated error and set it free.

Coup de grâce, a stroke of mercy, was not an unfamiliar expression. Moreover, I had seen it administered to a deer struck by a speeding car but not killed outright. But I had never applied the phrase or heard it applied to people.

"I don't think like this all the time—it kills me when I do," Naomi had written. But maybe there had to be a "killing," a wound of grace.

The natural man, the natural woman, the creature of the first spontaneity, does not choose pain and suffering. Thus joy and happiness have come to be images of good, of success, of blessing and benediction; and pain and suffering have come to be images of evil and of failure. The God of grace seems always to have been identified with progress and prosperity, even in men's warfaring! Only when a misfortune has an eventual and favorable issue do we speak of "a blessing in disguise."

Could our spiritual retardation be due to this correlation of happiness and success with God's grace, and pain and failure with God's punishment? Had I not witnessed with my own eyes the sterility and banality of those who in the eyes of the world "enjoyed uninterrupted good fortune?"

"God can't be lived like some serenely shining morning," the poet Rilke wrote. But people cling to the happiness and security of earth's abundance, and refuse the wound of grace that will take them far out and beyond immediacy, giving them pain and insecurity, perhaps even annihilating the "natural man and woman."

To refuse the wound of grace may be to refuse to be born again! To be born again is to go through the pain of dying to immediacy.

The creature of the first spontaneity conjugates her life according to the laws of feeling and possibility: "I have felt happy. I feel happy. I will go on feeling happy.

"I have felt secure. I feel secure. I will go on feeling secure."

In the face of minor frustrations and fears and afflictions, she convinces herself, "I have felt brave. I feel brave. I will go on feeling brave."

If she comes to a tougher, steeper uphill, she grits her teeth, and, like the little red engine in a child's story I had read many times to Naomi, she thinks brave, stouthearted, positive thoughts: "I think I can. I think I can. I think I can."

And maybe she can and maybe she does. But then, too, she may never learn to know her own true level of existence. She may never be stripped of her illusions about life, about others, about herself. She may never be detached from her finite attachments or disentangled from her transitory entanglements. A larger reality may never break into her present reality, if the life she is living can in all tolerance be called real.

In order to feel the fact of all that is mortal and finite, she who lives by feelings and on the strength of finite possibilities has to confront a dragon in her life—the dragon of impossibility. She needs to meet a situation where her brave little humanly powered red engine disintegrates on the tracks and with its last expiring breath pants: "I can't. I can't! It is impossible!"

In other words, she needs the wound of grace that makes her feel utterly unhappy, utterly insecure, utterly discouraged, utterly helpless.

The bankruptcy of her feelings and possibilities, the dissolution of her happy life of immediacy, may by the grace of the wound turn into a becoming. "Truth pierces matter where the heart is rent."

In my own salad days I had often secretly laughed at Sunday school teachers and Sunday preachers who prattled to my unreceptive ears, "We must needs pass through death that the old man may die." It was Pauline theology, of course, and not to my taste then. It took years of chewing Paul before I relished his taste.

But I suddenly realized there on the Rinsing Rock that Paul was speaking out of his own experience of a *coup de grâce* on the Damascus road. That expression "the old man," which had evoked nothing from me in my youth but giggles, meant the same as Kierkegaard's "the creature of the first spontaneity," the first-nature being who wants to remain forever young, forever happy, and forever secure in a world where aging, death, despair, and insecurity are built into the very fabric of life. First-nature being cannot bear the weight of such a world and must be annihilated—by a wound of grace.

"Well, Paul, you fierce old Jew," I chuckled as I climbed the cliff path with my laundry, minus one sheet, "Your 2,000-year-old theology explodes again and again as the freshest news out, and the fire-breathing dragon you met on the Damascus road turned out to be your Prince!"

A Dark Night of the Spirit

That night timber wolves howled on the ridge across the river and were answered by wolves in the clearing where the car was parked, a dozen deer-leaps from the cabin door. Wolf lovers insist that timber wolves are beautiful and noble animals and have their place in the northwoods system. Ignorance prevents me from joining the debate. All I can say is that nothing shatters one's illusion of her own courage and drives fear into the marrowbone faster than the nearby howling of timber wolves on a dark and moonless night when one is eight miles from another human being.

If the wolves had not been in the clearing, I would have made an abject and craven dash for the car and not stopped for three hundred miles until I was safely at home with my Partner. How utterly stupid to come to the cabin without him!

I hooked the door, pushed the woodbox against it, built up the fire in the fireplace, and huddled by the hearth. I gazed hypnotically into the fire, not daring to look at the windows lest I see there lewd, obscene eyes spurting jets of flame. I envisioned them leaping through the windows, and myself making my last stand with my back to the fire, holding them off for a while with a flaming broom, but eventually falling to their slavering jaws. The cabin would burn to the ground, and the local newspaper would report that I had perished in a cabin fire. No one would ever know the nature of my horrible death— no one!

If I survived the night, I would, of course, go home at the first streak of dawn. After carrying on a dialogue for a half hour, the wolves departed for other and distant ridges. As fear drained out of me, I was assailed by feelings of being a silly, foolish old woman, full of egotism and illusions about herself. Not only was I disillusioned with myself, I was disillusioned with the headway I thought I had been making in understanding pain and suffering and finding a meaning for Nani. Even the buoyant, new concept that had cost a sheet deflated in my mood of self-abnegation.

Was I to believe that Nani was a "wound of grace" sent to wean Naomi from the sap of youthful spontaneity before it inevitably dried up in the droughts and deserts of existential life? So that one person might have the possibility of becoming, would God create another that could never become a self even on the lowest level of consciousness? If so, did this not mean that pain and suffering, like the timber wolves, were part of a prescribed system, that Nani's part in the system was similar to that of the tender fawn destined for the wolf pack?

Did the God of grace use pain and suffering to *torment* people into fruitful self-torment? Was God, like Socrates and Kierkegaard, scornful of the unexamined life, so scornful that he bent and broke people on the rack of pain and suffering just to make contemplatives of them? If so, what of the rank and file who would bend and break and never become contemplatives? What was better—to rot in the unexamined life or to bend and break under afflictions? Did only philosophers and Einsteins inhabit the kingdom?

Furthermore, if the purpose of pain and suffering is to detach us from finite things and train us for the life of the spirit in God, then comfort and consolation are not only inappropriate but downright detrimental! Consolation that softens the bitterness may prevent us from fleeing to God's grace. Applying the salve of sympathy to the wound of grace may seal up the opening through which grace may pass. If this is true, then as far as spiritual life is concerned an ounce of non-intervention might be worth a being-born-again or a transition into the Second Spontaneity. An ounce of compassion might mean the loss of the kingdom, the continent of Yes, and a descent to the non-kingdom, the subcontinent of No.

Are all the laws in the kingdom, that Yes-Continent of the spirit, *inverse?* Is black white there? Is up down and down up, a loss gain and a gain loss, pain a good and pleasure a harm, a crushed and comfortless life good and a pleasant and profitable life bad?

For two days my mind had been chafing and fretting at the border of the continent of Yes, like Moses standing on the border of the Promised Land and permitted only a glimpse of it. I did not have forty years to spend in the wilderness! With no evidence as yet to witness for the Yes-Continent and all these subversive thoughts witnessing against it, I wondered that night if I had not been led down a dead-end street, if I had not been cruelly bamboozled or self-deluded. Was what I had thought to be the testimony of Spirit to my spirit only the testimony of my heightened self? What, if anything, did all this enlightenment on the river have to do with my originally simple desire to have a simple explanation for innocent suffering?

What had begun as a dark night of terror had turned into a dark night of the spirit. I put another log on the fire and decided to spend the rest of the night in a sleeping bag on the floor before the fireplace.

"But even the dark night of the spirit may be a form of grace," I whispered to myself much later, and before I fell into deep sleep I knew that it was indeed so. I knew that these painful and confusing questions were a gift of grace to my spirit, sent to prevent there being anything maudlin, namby-pamby, pedantic, smug, or even dogmatic in my "simple explanation of innocent suffering."

No Gospel of Suffering

Dawn sprouted in the dark soil of night, un-furled its tendrils, and was day in full flower before I awoke. Instead of going home, I put a book in a small backpack and took the path I had made to the gorge down the river.

Fording the river at the end of my path, where the cliff rose sheer and steep a hundred feet or more, I was able to enter the canyon where the river began to fall in a series of waterfalls. From the logs and beaver-chewed chunks and driftwood thrown high at the turn of the river, one can see that at high spring-flood time the gorge is full of river.

Now, in the middle of a rather dry June, I was able to wade through forking streams and establish myself on dry bedrock in the middle of the cascading waters just above the largest waterfall.

I think I must have sat for a full hour feasting on the festival banquet for all my senses—the black cliff splashed with orange lichen, the sun-warmed saddle of stone on which I sat, the cool spray blown back on me from the falls by an upstream breeze, the aroma of balsam and spruce growing on the high banks, and the symphony of the river.

A span of but twelve hours between a state of fear and trembling and a state of inebriate rapture! Now I was in no mood to search out a gospel of suffering in the book I had brought to the gorge. But, obedient to my pursuit, I finally began to read to see if, after all my stalking other books and stalling on this one, I could find anything in the four Gospels to illuminate our common lot in the world.

I read, and mused, and read, and mused some more—until I became completely oblivious to the beauty around me.

Matthew 1:1. The book of the genealogy of Jesus Christ, the son of David, the son of Abraham . . .

Luke 2:7. And she gave birth to her first-born son and wrapped him in swaddling cloths, and laid him in a manger, because there was no place for them in the inn.

It is not true that you went into eclipse after creating the universe and human life, and let your creation go its own capricious way. You did once thrust yourself omnipotently into the human scene and placed your eternal "I Am" into the seed of a woman with a genealogy. You made her cry with the pain of your birthing and the joy "that a child is born

into the world." You curtailed and caged your om-
nipresence to a speck of space in your universe,
abridged your Eternal Self to the time space of one
human life cut down in the prime of young man-
hood. You let yourself be born nude and native into
the nullity and cruelty and rottenness of life in this
world. You made yourself indigenous to the Absurd,
the life that extends from contradiction to contradiction to death.

For it was not only the "Gloria in Excelsis"
that heralded your birth. It was also the lamentation
of all the Jewish mothers of all the boy babies two
and under slain by King Herod in Bethlehem and its
environs:

> *A voice was heard in Ramah,*
> *wailing and loud lamentation,*
> *Rachel weeping for her children;*
> *she refused to be consoled,*
> *because they were no more.*

Matthew 4:1. Then Jesus was led up by the
Spirit into the wilderness to be tempted by the devil.
And he fasted forty days and forty nights, and after-
ward he was hungry.

Forty days and forty nights, and not a word
from Matthew about your physical suffering during
that fast, except to say matter-of-factly "and afterward he was hungry." If that were today the news
reporters would have spun each detail into columns

of print, for the more we the public regard personal suffering as embarrassing, distressing, and unendurable, the more avid and morbid we are to hear and read accounts of the sufferings of others. "Suffering" stories are to adults like horror stories to children.

Gospels make it plain that you were not suffering for a public, not even as an example to a public. It was a purely voluntary personal suffering. Why? Was it a tool, a means to an end? A girding for action? Was it a meaningful way to train your body to bear the pains of the future? Was it your way of mastering your body so that you would no longer have to struggle with its passions and pressures, so that you could go without food and water and sleep, if need be? So that you could endure the passions and pressures of a man's sexuality? Was it simply and solely to empty your body of all desires so that you could make those three tremendous affirmations without one reluctant, grudging, negative fraction of your self whispering, "No!"

> *Man shall not live by bread alone, but by every word that proceeds from the mouth of God.*
> *You shall not tempt the Lord your God.*
> *You shall worship the Lord your God and him only shall you serve.*

It is the affirmations the Gospel writers find important, hence no morbid details to arouse maudlin pity for the suffering Jesus and no whys and wherefores for the suffering. Not a hint of the beginning of a gospel of suffering here.

Matthew 9:35–37: And Jesus went about all the cities and villages, teaching in their synagogues, and preaching the gospel of the kingdom, and healing every disease and every infirmity. When he saw the crowds, he had compassion for them, because they were harassed and helpless, like sheep without a shepherd.

I felt the wingbeat of a thought, but read on.

Matthew 11:2–6: Now when John heard in prison about the deeds of Christ, he sent word by his disciples and said to him, "Are you he who is to come, or shall we look for another?" And Jesus answered them, "Go and tell John what you hear and see: the blind receive their sight and the lame walk, lepers are cleansed and the deaf hear, and the dead are raised up, and the poor have good news preached to them. And blessed is he who takes no offense at me."

Who are you, Jesus—an Author, tasting human misery for the sake of experiences that will go into a book he plans to write about suffering?

Are you the Sage and Founder of a School of Suffering, walking about in sandals, reciting its gospel among the poor and lowly and suffering of the world?

Are you the bearded Social Activist agonizing over the problem of suffering and railing on the street corners against the injustices and wickedness that cause suffering?

Are you the Preacher denouncing this accursed present generation and ascribing all suffering to its sinfulness?

Are you the Government Fact Finder making a study of human needs in a given area with a view to drafting a new program to be called ACTION?

Are you the Knight of Resignation and Despair going around and making the most of a rotten situation?

You are none of these! You are simply and solely God's I Am incarnate in the flesh. When you accepted human form, you accepted evil and suffering as a fact of life in this world. The alchemy of No, of nonacceptance, produces hatred, hostility, harshness, bitterness, malice. The alchemy of your Yes to existential suffering produced a compassion such as the world has never seen, a life of living, loving, and giving such as the world has never known. You wasted no time agonizing over the great wound of pain and suffering in creation or in asking who dealt this wound. You simply accepted it as the mystery of existence and then devoted your life to healing it.

The crowd read in your eyes God's love for them in their miserable condition and flocked to you.

The crowd laid bare its painful, suffering wound, and you touched the wound with your hand, your most personal human hand—and healed it.

No gospel of suffering in the Gospels, then— just you—God's Yes to a suffering world. No illumination of pain and suffering in the Gospels—just you, God's I Am Love radiantly and utterly illuminated.

No, Not One!

My return from the gorge to the cabin should have been made in a celebrant mood, for I truly believed that, like the Old Woman with her pig, I had gotten over the stile and could get home—if not that night, then the next. Reflecting on the life of Jesus had convinced me that the question of pain and suffering can be answered only in one's own life.

Suffering was, is, and will always remain a mystery. It cannot be explained or solved with words. In fact, giving theoretical answers may lead to the conclusion that the problem has been solved.

The mystery of pain and suffering can only be answered with a life that refuses to despair, refuses to hand one more victory over to the forces of No, but instead makes itself an instrument of Yes, gives itself in love and compassion to alleviate pain and suffering. We may be driven to speculate upon, brood over, agonize over the problem of suffering, but ultimately and essentially we are to make ourselves instruments of its alleviation. This is what Jesus did. This is what we are to do. This is what I must do. This is what Naomi, awakened to misery and to mercy, must do.

The only symbolic act I could think of then and there to signalize this new meaning was to dip my cup into the river and water the ferns nature was trying to grow in the tiny fissure gardens of huge boulders. With no subsoil and no rain for two weeks, the ferns were curling against their first unfurling, and their newborn green was edged with brown.

But there was a maggot in my mood! My mind seemed to be satisfied with this newest and fullest meaning—but not my spirit. The darkness of pain and suffering had been greatly illuminated here on the river, especially today in the gorge, but there was still an unilluminated darkness that could be felt by my spirit. By the time I arrived at the cabin door, I knew what it was.

The illumination to which my mind had said "Yes" in the gorge had been light upon the *life* of Christ. Yet all four Gospels march swiftly, deliberately, and with dry eyes to the cross. Apparently on eternity's scale the death of Christ far outweighs the life of Christ! In my pondering there in the gorge I had simply taken the death on the cross to be the overwhelming and culminating proof of Christ's love and compassion for human kind. Any other ending would have been unequal to the life.

It would be like having Hamlet marry a Swedish princess and become King of Denmark and father of a robust royal family; or Joan of Arc being rescued by an ardent admirer just as the flames licked at her garments and being carried away to a long and happy life in a castle on the Rhone.

I shut the cabin door behind me, leaned against it, and closed my eyes. "All my life I have been taught and told, O Christ, that you had to die on the cross to make reparation to a God who demanded justice for a rebellious creation. The very idea appalled me—and still does. The cross has always been scandalous to my mind and repulsive to my emotions— and still is. Long ago I pushed that meaning away as utterly offensive. If the time has come for me to sit up and pay attention to it, and if you are trying to tell me that your death can illuminate the darkness of pain and suffering even more than your life, then knock at my brain house. I suddenly find myself willing to listen, although I doubt that I can ever believe it."

And then began what was not self-communing, but more than a heightened consciousness and less than a mystical experience. I like to call it a cerebral happening, and it happens when both my consciousness and subconsciousness have wrapped their sinewy arms and legs around a question and hold it captive to my attention. It happens when I have opened wide all the doors and windows of my being to any breeze, faint drumbeat, or scent or gleam of perception. It becomes a kind of running dialogue that is completely undiscriminating as to time and place. It takes place at any hour, in and out of bed, over an ironing board, while weeding the garden, washing the dishes. As I recall it, the dialogue that late afternoon and evening happened something like this.

Place: The springbarrel, where I am dipping water into a pail.

NOT-I: Suppose that, in a new and thrilling dimension of compassion and dedication to a cause, we were able to heal all the sick and blind and dumb, clothe all the poor, and feed all the hungry in the world. Suppose that we were able to correct all the economic and political conditions that cause poverty, inequity, and wretchedness. Would that put an end to pain and suffering?

I: I am sure that it would not.

NOT-I: Then there must be deeper roots for suffering than natural infirmities (including your granddaughter's brain damage). There must be deeper roots than economic insecurity and political injustice. Where are these deeper roots that would not be touched even by realizing the ideal of health, wealth, liberty, and equality for all?

I: They are internal in us, not external.

Place: Under the dark tent of the huge evergreen by the spring path where I always set down the pail to rest.

NOT-I: You just set down a heavy burden on a steep path. If human beings were able to set down their heaviest burden of suffering on the path of life, it would be the consciousness of their sins.

I (*vehemently, and picking up my pail so abruptly that I slosh water on my feet*): Not so! Now you're talking Sunday pulpit-prattle. We moderns do *not* feel especially burdened by sin, and if you want the plain truth, we yawn over the cross!

Place: The cabin, where I am putting on dry socks.

NOT-I (*obviously trying another approach*): In this tiny little community of cabins where you and your close friends have brought your families in July and August for some twenty years, you are the one who knows the woods and river better than any of them.

In your own mind you think of yourself as a combination of a barefoot dryad of the forests and a river nymph. (*I nod uncertainly, not knowing whether I should feel guilty or proud.*) While the children sported in the river, you went off by yourself. You all came back to the cabin about the same time. Do you remember how you felt as you came back?

I: Ecstatic! Beatific! At one with God, with fellow humans, and with nature! Every string of my being in tune!

NOT-I: How long did this inner harmony last?

I: Until the first one in the family played out of tune or someone in the community irritated or frustrated me.

NOT-I: Then your little community of family and friends does not operate according to the laws of love, which are the universal laws of being?

I: What family, what community does?

NOT-I: Why have you always been the pathmaker, the woodgatherer, the watergetter in this wilderness community? Why have you all your life chosen tasks that give you solitude?

I (*beginning to understand*): Because I long to feel at one, in harmony, whole not fractured, complete not incomplete, united not disunited.

NOT-I: When you are in solitude, you sometimes fantasize, day-dream situations and relationships. At such times does your imagination create harmony or disharmony, unity or disunity?

I: Always coherence, always completeness, always wholeness, always oneness!

NOT-I: Do you have *one* actual, rather than fantasized, human relationship that you can say is complete, harmonious, unbroken, and continuous? Where you feel completely at one with the other? A relationship of transparent love and joy?

I: No, not one!

NOT-I: Why are you crying?

I (*savagely*): Because I have so recently been deprived of my last illusion of such a friendship! The wound is still raw.

NOT-I: Would you call it anguish?

I: Yes, it qualifies as anguish—the anguish of alienation, loneliness, of not being in relationship. A void where I was so sure there was a touching of spirits.

NOT-I: Whose was the fault? Whose the flaw?

I: Mine as well as the other's.

This ended the dialogue that night, because when both the consciousness and subconsciousness wrap themselves around self-pity and the I is wholly engrossed in feeling sorry for itself, dialogue with any other is impossible.

Backed to the Wall

But the dialogue began again the moment I opened my eyes the next morning. In fact, it was as if Not-I had waited patiently at the door of consciousness the entire night and came in with the sound of the river and the chill of the morning. I curled up in the warm nest of blankets and decided to carry on this dialogue in bed for a while.

I: You became a bit too personal last night.

NOT-I: The roots of pain and suffering are deep in the person. This is where pain and suffering have to be addressed.

I: Well, you touched rock-bottom last night: the alienation that I share with every human being, the impossibility of an unbroken, continuous relationship of transparent love and joy, the anguish of this alienation. For the deepest human longing and need is for such a relationship.

NOT-I: Are you sure that alienation is the rock-bottom anguish of the human spirit? Suppose that people, spurred on by sensational new knowledge about the human mind, were able to alter undesirable behavior patterns and produce a better humanity. What if they could really liberate people from the contradictions of their subliminal selves and make them ethical heroes of a sort—filled with noble, selfless sentiments, impatient with mediocrity and self-seeking, disdaining money, renouncing personal ambition, working with singleness of mind and religious zeal to transform profoundly the world and achieve a temporal salvation for human kind. Suppose by incredible vitality and selfless involvement they were to achieve this ideal; suppose they could in fact live lives of compassion as close to the life Jesus lived on this earth as is humanly possible. Would that put an end to pain and suffering?

I (*so vehemently that I leaped out of bed and was quite oblivious to the cabin cold*): No! For they would know the pain and suffering of inevitable failure. Why do you plague me with such thoughts? After all, I am living in the last half of the twentieth century, the most convincing evidence against any theory of progress. I know what you are trying to do: corner me into a consciousness of sin! But you won't ever catch me in the sin of optimism—be it Marxist Utopianism or the American Great Society!

Place: Two hours later, sawing and chopping wood outside the sauna

I: What you were trying to lead me to see, of course, was that there is a deeper root to our pain and suffering than disharmony, and that even if we achieved the impossible and cured that disharmony, we would still know pain and suffering. The Church says this is because we face eternal damnation. But something in me protests this stress on saving my own soul, on getting myself saved for eternity. This emphasis on the beyond does not appeal to me. I have no particular yen to be everlasting. As for the "making my peace with my Maker" approach, I feel, like Thoreau, that we have never really quarreled.

NOT-I: You seem to have experienced the joy and bliss of close human relationships, of being related to a person in a love that is transparent and without judgment, accepting the other's whole being in joy, and feeling yourself accepted by the other in the same way.

I: Yes, there have been some such relationships in my life, but they never remained so simple, lucid, honest, and open.

NOT-I: You do, however, deeply desire them to remain so. You do long to have these relationships be continuous, unbroken, unchanged?

I: Yes, these relationships that stir the roots of my whole being to April joy—I do truly desire them to remain forever April. But they never do! They remain relationships, but they become cloudy and November.

NOT-I: Do you believe in God as Eternal Spirit and Being who created you to be spirit and being with whom he may live in a relationship that stirs the roots of your whole self, awakens you to the possibility of becoming what he created you to be? A relationship where you know that God loves you utterly—and utterly as you are—in fact, loves you for the you-ness of you, the special, particular, individual, personal, unique, original you-ness of you?

I (*startled*): You make him sound like a lover!

NOT-I: Which he is.

I: What about the judge part?

NOT-I: People never come before a judge as committees, clubs, crowds, or congregations—always as single individuals. In this sense God is called a judge, for we live our lives before him as individuals, accountable to him as single, solitary individuals:

I (*firmly*): Yes, I do believe in God who is spirit who created me spirit to live in relationship with him.

NOT-I: Is your relationship to God one of transparent love and joy, unbroken and continuous?

I: Sometimes I feel that it is, and sometimes I feel that it isn't. (*I stop short, silenced by the illogic of my answer.*) All right, it is *not* unbroken and continuous. It is very episodic.

NOT-I: Do you anguish that it is episodic?

I (*throwing the ax in a fury*): Will you shut up and leave me alone! And what in heaven or hell does this have to do with Nani!

Yes, Yes, Yes!

A half hour later in the sauna, where I had built a small fire and lay on the top shelf looking out the window at the river, the dialogue resumed.

I (*humbly*): Why is it so episodic? Why do I feel "in relationship" for three weeks, maybe, and "out of relationship" for six months? Now don't tell me it's because I have never been converted, never accepted Christ, never thrown myself at the Throne of Grace, etcetera, etcetera.

NOT-I: You have never accepted the death of Christ on the cross for your sins.

I (*angrily*): Here we are, right back where we started! I repeat that I do not feel particularly sinful! I happen to be living in an age of relativities, and by the relativities in which we now live I am relatively adequate.

NOT-I: You agree that God is a God of love and that the laws of being are the laws of love.

I: Yes, wholeheartedly. I can even recite it. Luke 10:27: "You shall love the Lord your God with all your heart, and with all your soul, and with all your strength, and with all your mind; and your neighbor as yourself."

NOT-I: Would you agree that God's law of love is absolute? You do not accuse yourself of murder, theft, or unchastity, but do you ever accuse yourself of not having loved enough? Or do you feel that you love quite adequately?

I: I never said that!

NOT-I: But you did! (*After a long silence*) I know what you are doing: making a catalogue of particular times when you did not live by the absolute law of love. You are making a list of specific people whom you do not love by the absolute law of love.

But God is not interested in your particulars, only in your condition; for the particulars are the result of the condition. It is your condition that is sin, and the particulars are the consequences of the condition. The condition is infinitely worse than the particulars. The lynching of a black man is not as sinful as the condition that caused it. Long before the lynching the condition clamored for the act.

Stop thinking of the hostile and disturbed girl you did not take into your home when it appeared that she would be disruptive and would require much more attentive love and time than you felt you had to give. Think instead of the condition that prompted that guilty No. Think of the dark No that lives within you, that battles to be the master passion of your spirit.

I: OK, you win. My condition is such that I can never love God or other human beings as God requires me to love. Therefore I am alienated from both God and humans. Therefore I anguish. This is the secret root of human despair, of our pain and suffering! Now are you satisfied? Well, I am not! My mind still boggles at the cross.

NOT-I: Think of a relationship to the person of God in the most superlative human terms you know, it would still be woefully inadequate. Think of it as a relationship where you are ever becoming. It is not a relationship devoid of pain and suffering, but even the pain and suffering are turned into instruments of your becoming. Knowing such a relationship, would you wish it to be terminated at your death? Could you face an eternity of no relationship, of Nothingness? Does not your whole being deeply long that such a relationship—which here on earth you know only in part—be a perpetual union, unbroken, continuous, and unchanged?

I: Oh yes! A dying into nothingness, losing such a relationship, would be—hell!

NOT-I: This is why Christ died on the cross and was raised again, absurd as it seems. Had he merely lived

a life of pure compassion here on earth, you would
not have the possibility of this eternal relationship to
the Eternal. Had he merely died, he would not have
given you the possibility of this eternal relationship
to God. God had to assume human existence broad-
ly, all its absurdity, all its pain, all its suffering, all
its terror. God had to experience being bent and broken, had to know the absolute despair of alienation
and forsakenness. Christ had to cry from the shud-
dering depths of his being the human cry of despair,
alienation, and aloneness: "My God, my God, why
hast Thou forsaken me?" He had to belong so entirely to the human rottenness present in the Absurd
that he had to die as a sinner on a criminal's gibbet
for the human condition of sin. He had to taste in
time the bitterness of eternal isolation from God so
that you may have eternal relationship with him. To
bridge the abyss between time and eternity he had to
descend into the abyss.

I: It still sounds like a scheme hatched below and not
in the heavenly courts of love!

NOT-I: If it had been a scheme hatched below, it
would not have involved suffering and death on a
cross. The hero that the mastermind of the subcontinent of No would advance would not be a suffering
servant. He would be a colossal hero—if not in fact,
then in fiction; for the Madison Avenue of the capital
city of No would cunningly construct a colossal im-

age for their savior of the human race. Shrewd as he is, the mastermind of No cannot conceive of a redeemer who is as penniless and powerless as a beggar, who suffers and dies the shockingly ignominious death meted out to the most despicable enemies of society.

I (*whispering*): The inverse laws of spirit.

NOT-I: Right! In a way the cross is a de-creation, a shattering of human values. For it was not a great ethical hero triumphantly testing his soul and endurance who died on the cross, but the Son of God testifying in his human nature to human misery—and in his divine nature testifying that God loves his creation immersed in its misery.

I: Stop right there! I still cannot see how the cross affects our misery here and now. And don't forget my Nani and my Naomi!

NOT-I: The cross affects our misery here and now by curing the self-loathing and despair that eat at the marrowbone of the human spirit. The human spirit knows what the human mind may not know. (Incidentally, what the mind knows does not seem to exercise much influence on our lives.) The human spirit knows self-loathing, because the human spirit knows that it completely fails to live by the eternal laws of love. The human spirit knows *despair,* because the human spirit knows that it is impossible to live by the eternal laws of love, and therefore cannot hope or expect to live in relationship to the God of love, and therefore has lost relationship to the God of love, now and for all eternity. The human spirit knows this even if the mind does not.

But the God of love says, "Yes, I offer you the possibility of unbroken relationship. Here on the cross in the broken body of my son is my offer of unbroken relationship to me. Here is my 'Yes, you are forgiven.' Here is my guarantee of a totally new relationship, a new creation—faith, faith in my beloved son. The opposite of sin and despair is no longer virtue; it is faith in my son."

If God's Yes incarnate in the flesh had not suffered, you who suffer would feel superior to him. You would in your superiority say No to him. Do not pass lightly over that cry, "My God, my God, why hast Thou forsaken me?" It is that cry of desolation, that cry out of the temporary eclipse of God, the silence of God, the darkness of no dialogue—it is that cry that draws you out of your own darkness. That cry silences the spirit of No in you, the spirit of defiance and despair. It summons forth your Yes.

I: Yes to what?

NOT-I: Not to a body of affirmations, not to a new patchwork, not to a new program of action, not to a new struggle to be virtuous and worthy, but Yes to him who suffered and died on the cross for your sinful condition.

And I? I had not a word more to say. There on the top shelf of the sauna I skimmed the Gospels once more in the light of this most recent illumination, and it was there all right, just as Not-I had said!

I have come that men may have life
and have it in its fullness.
I am the way.
I am the truth.
I am the door.
I am the true vine.
I am the resurrection and the life.
Unless a grain of wheat falls into the earth
and dies, it remains alone:
but if it dies it bears much fruit.

Late that night, I, who all my life had said Yes to the life of Christ but had never really said Yes to his death on the cross, said a most ungrudging Yes to that, too. Having done so, I did not experience any mystical exaltation, not even a vivid relief. I did not shout "Hallelujah" to the rafters, but deep down where the meanings are, and deeper still, where the spirit is, there was a brightening and an eastering that had not been there before.

No Difference at All!

I awoke the next morning to what I knew would be my last day on the river until my Partner and I returned in July and the children and grand-children filtered back for their too short vacations. The cup of Lake Superior we can see from our high point on the river was Copenhagen blue.

Knowing that the sun would stay the day, I descended to the river with a pillow and a book and settled down on the Giantess' Lap.

Whenever I experience any kind of a significant illumination of a blurred, confused meaning, I skim Scripture from Genesis to Revelation and let this new light fall on the "old stuff." It never fails, and it did not fail today; the "old stuff" became as modern as my most recent heartbeat. The whole Old Testament was the story of my own spiritual life, responding to external events rather than being directed by and from an internal event, responding in ecstasy to glorious happenings, feeling dull, dead, and despondent when there were none. Sometimes yeasty and buoyant, sometimes sour and dull. Always episodic.

When Moses came down from Mount Sinai the skin of his face shone because he had been talking with God.

But the skin-glow of Word-flame faded; the bright alive of oneness gloomed. Thereafter was ever thus: a descent into the existential, an eclipse of rapture.

Afterward was always a slow dissolving, a glow-setting. The afterglow was nice while it lasted, Lord God; but it always died in your silence until— until you put your whole self into your Word, until your Word became flesh and blood and lived among us, until that flesh was torn and that blood was shed for us, until talking with you was no longer a matter of climbing a mountain to you, but of you descending to us until you conversed with us in your Son and on the cross.

In Christ the Son
Nows of glow
Glows of Now
Eternal Now
Eternal Glow.

Halfway through the Gospels, I stopped my swift skimming, laughed aloud, and struck the ancient boulder with the palms of my hands. "O, you Rock of my Salvation, all those stale old cliches are true. O ye angels, archangels, seraphim, and cherubim, don't swoon or faint there in your invisible kingdom, but I feel like shouting a song to the river, a song that has veritably embarrassed me all my life!"

Spirit-tippled and Word-bibbed, I did sing there on the river with gusto:

Just as I am, without one plea,
But that Thy blood was shed for me,
And that Thou bid'st me come to Thee,
O Lamb of God, I come, I come!

After that bit of wholly satisfying intemperance, I moved to the Table Rock and lay for a long time looking down into the river.

The thought came to me that somewhere recently I had read about the discovery of an ancient scroll containing sayings ascribed to Jesus not recorded in the four Gospels. One of them, as I recalled it, was, "Turn over any stone, and I am there."

Figuratively, at least, the words were true. I had turned over the heavy stone of the pain and suffering of Nani and had found Christ there. I had a feeling that any painful problem, the front side of any question at which one stares fixedly, has the same backside.

Turn it over, and there one finds Christ. The frontsides of questions may be different. The backsides are always the same. "Turn over any stone, and I am there."

But Nani was, is, and will remain a burden and a source of pain. Moreover, she could never even begin to comprehend any of the meanings that had come to me here on the river. What grace was there for her—*directly*—in all this grace? Oh, I knew there were hosts of "indirectly's," and they would be flocking into my mind very soon. But directly?

If Naomi had lived contemporaneously with Jesus Christ of Nazareth, she would have brought her baby to him, and he would have taken Nani in his arms, put his hand upon her head, and healed her directly. But what direct thing could he do for Nani now? Or for all the others who could never rise on the intellectual scale above idiocy? Or those who in the senility of old age had gradually slid down the scale of intelligence to imbecility and vacuity?

I thought of the father of a dear friend, a vigorous, intelligent, gifted leader of the church who in his last years became so *absent*-minded that he simply lay and babbled numbers. Is being absent-in-mind synonymous with being absent-in-spirit?

To have faith do we need to have enough mind to grasp the meaning of faith? To be in the relationship of faith to God, do we need a measurable IQ?

A vehement "No!" brought me to my feet. I threw a stone so hard against Gog that it bounced to Magog, and on each boulder raised a smoke that floated back to my nostrils with the acrid smell of an exploded firecracker.

The meaning of life is in the relationship of the whole person to God, not in the relationship of the cerebellum. The relationship to God is possible in Christ for every individual from Einstein—to Nani. In pity and sympathy people go down to a certain level of intelligence to admit fellow-beings to their self-made heavens, but then disgust, horror, and scorn take over and say, "No, such a non-human as you cannot come in." But God's love descends lower and takes the lowest. Indeed, his eyes see no difference at all between an Einstein and a cretin.

I thought of my friend's father.

> When the tenuous tape
> coiled on the reel of his memory
> no longer tensible
> broke
> and in his patching and repairing
> he fused incompatible pieces,
>
> When the tenacious thread of memory
> frayed and flaccid
> slackened, bunched, knotted
> and finally unravelled
> into a tortuous, twisted tangle,
>
> When others heard the twang of breaking memory
> and saw the shattered fragments of what was mind
> and murmured sorrowfully,
> "How tragic!

He was a giant in his day!"

The Lord God picked up the fumbled, jumbled words
the topsy-turvey alphabet
the whole embarrassing litter
and it was as if they rearranged themselves
into a liturgy of praise!

And it was so.
The Lord God looked
and, behold, it was very good.

When the contours of ideas blurred and eclipsed
the colors of emotions faded out
and words themselves grew
vague and meaningless,
when even word-sounds
vowels and consonants
retained no meaning,

When—strangely—
as he lay in his long dying—
numbers became his living language
and he intoned them one by one
tirelessly
hour upon hour
day after day
as time tallied its final count for him,

When others stood beside his bed
and heard his babbling numbers
and tiptoed tearfully away,

The Lord God gathered up the digits and the ciphers
the sum total of his numbers
the whole untidy chaos
and they added up!

and their sum was—adoration!

And it was so.
The Lord God looked
and, behold, it was very good.

When, finally,
he lay in a dimension that was no dimension
in the deep beyond and far behind of
subconsciousness,

When eyes betrayed no flutter of thought
and all that stirred in him
was feeble, faltering breath
and tired faithful heart,

When others could not bear to see
and called what they saw
"just existing,"

The Lord God looked into the abandoned house
where not even dried autumn leaves drifted,
shifted absurdly
across the bleached warped floor.
The Lord God saw
not the empty vastness
but the vast givenness
that was and is and evermore shall be!

And it was so.
The Lord God looked
and, behold, it was very good.

As I had expected, hosts of "indirectly's" began crowding into my mind on the heels of this direct meaning for Nani. But I dismissed them politely and asked them to wait for the long drive home the next day. I had a task to do, a promise to Naomi to keep. It was to put her beloved river in a box and send it to her.

Into the plastic-lined box, which I airmailed the next day, went ten rust-red, blue-gray smooth pebbles, nine tablespoons of the rich mold of a perished pine, eight tiny fairy cups in a bed of moss, seven bark "grotesques" designed by the river, and weathered by the sun, six bright green cones of an evergreen, five "stars of the north," the flowers of the bunchberry, four tablespoons of amber water from the river, three curls of birch bark, two tiny ferns, one microscopic cedar tree.

An Eagle in the Soul

After locking the cabin door, I went to the river to say goodbye and, of course, I was beguiled to linger—to sun, to swim, and even to lie on my favorite rock, and read my favorite author. In the seventh chapter I found the fitting words of farewell.

I had come to the river in the mood of Psalm 42:

> I say to God, my rock:
> "Why hast thou forgotten me?
> Why go I mourning
> because of the oppression of the enemy?"

> As with a deadly wound in my body,
> my adversaries taunt me
> while they say to me continually,
> "Where is your God?"

> Why are you cast down, O my soul,
> and why are you disquieted within me?
> Hope in God; for I shall again praise him,
> my help and my God.

I left the river with John's words singing in my
ears like the symphony of the river:

On the last day of the feast, the great day,
Jesus stood up and proclaimed,
"If any one thirst, let him come to me
and drink. He who believes in me, as
the scripture has said, 'Out of his heart
shall flow rivers of living water.'"
Now this he said about the Spirit,
which those who believed in him
were to receive.

So that was how the third member of the Trinity fit in! God, the rock of steadfast love before
whom our human love is but a grain of sand. Christ,
the living water, in whom we have forgiveness of sins,
in whom, buoyant and free, we can float in the existential life of contradictions and suffering. And Spirit, poured into our human spirits to help us say our
weak and faltering Yes, flowing out of our spirits a
river of living water to bathe and lave the pain and
suffering of the world.

"O, you Reality, so aptly pictured by rocks,
living water, and flowing streams! No wonder I love
this white water river!" I thought, and slid once more
into the parable of the river to float buoyantly and
swim boldly in its waters, at ease and quite at home.

After mailing the box of river at the first post
office on the shore (so that the gift would have an

"up north" postmark), I drove the three hundred miles home without stopping. As I had fully expected, the thoughts still trooped in, which meant that the attention of my whole being was still centered on the question of pain and suffering.

Some were No thoughts, but this, too, I expected and will continue to expect until I die into the utterly illumined kingdom of Yes. But since there was no longer any possibility of the No forces taking over my spirit, I did not tremble and despair before them any more. I simply let my Yes answer them.

NO: Why the elation? Was it such a big deal up there on the river? After all, pain is still pain, and suffering is still suffering, and Nani is still Nani.

YES: True, pain is still pain, and suffering is still suffering, and Nani is still Nani, but the deepest root of human suffering is cut by the cross, and the human spirit is released from its worst anxiety and dread: anxiety about death, the dread of dying into nothingness, total extinction, dying into total and permanent isolation from the eternal God. To be released from suffering that dread about eternity sets one free for the struggle in time.

NO: What struggle?

YES: Against *you!* Against your forces of No within and without that create most of the pain and suffering in this life.

(A detour for road construction and a trailing traffic cop silenced the dialogue for a time, but it resumed again.)

NO: We are uncomfortably aware, some of us, that a revolution is taking place, but it seems to us that you Christians in the past have been so interested in the "beyond" and in saving your own souls that you have been callous to injustice and indifferent to suffering other than your own. We have a cynical saying that no one dies of another's wound, and we don't see many of you dying or even suffering for another's wound. We, of course, rejoice in the fact.

YES: I would be the last to deny that. It is the sin of Christendom that we live and die as if Christ suffered and died to provide us with a cozy, untroubled life and a peaceful death. But the Spirit is always convicting us of that sin. (Please note that the Church is constantly being healed from within!) The Spirit is always producing suffering servants who refuse to despair over the world, who do not isolate themselves from human pain and suffering, but say: "Life is absurd; we are part of it. The world is full of pain and suffering; it is ours." And to the degree that they accept life's absurdity and pain, to that same degree they offer their lives to alleviate human misery.

Then I myself, speaking for myself, said aloud, in a "try and top this" spirit, "And they love God in and through and beyond their own sufferings. They curse neither the pain nor God for allowing it. They simply offer their lives to it, and they praise. Francis of Assisi did not curse leprosy; he kissed the leper and praised God. Martin Luther King did not curse the cancer of racism; he walked in the streets with his suffering brothers and sisters—and praised God!"

The voice of No was silenced for a time, but it came back for one last attempt to stir up distress in my spirit, addressing me directly, not my Yes.

NO: What about Nani? What about Naomi? I suppose now that you have thought so hard about this matter, you will feel obliged to lecture, sermonize, moralize.

I: A frightful temptation! But Naomi will have to do as every human has to do: confront the stark truths of self, confront pain and suffering, confront the cross—all by herself. She will have to discover for herself whether she loves God on the level of a family of lovely, lively, bright children, or deeper down, farther back, and behind that. I shall continue to pray that she not be plunged into a nightmare, that she accept the suffering and through it is awakened to mercy, love, and joy.

NO: I'm curious. What is the first thing you will do about the problem when you get home?

I: In the first place I shall no longer call Nani a problem—or, for that matter, any source of pain and suffering that has no solution. Such pain and suffering is a mystery. A problem is like that road block back there, something that looms up before the self, obstructing its passage, frustrating and interfering with its normal progress, spoiling the self's pleasant life.

One fine day the problem, like that road block, may not be there; the whole clumsy obstruction may be gone. But a mystery—a mystery is not simply a barrier that looms up before the self, some big negative something to be pushed away or put back where it was. Nor is it a heavy something on top of the self, a huge boulder crushing the self. A mystery is something that the self finds itself caught up into.

The self can never really see the mystery in its entirety, know it in its fullness, because the self is not outside of it but is within it, is a part of it. Or the mystery may be said to be within the self. Since the mystery is within the self, it does not paralyze the self or make it motionless. It sets the self in motion.

Please understand that this is not a self-starting, self-propelling motion. It is the power of the divine Yes leading the self to say Yes to the suffering. Even though the self may continue to be a suffering self, in and through the power of the divine Yes it becomes a serving self, a loving self. It addresses the mystery of pain and suffering with its life.

NO: Ha! I thought you were not going to lecture, sermonize, or moralize.

I: I said I would not lecture, sermonize, or moralize to Naomi, but, believe me, whenever you or any other voice of No begins to badger me, I shall clobber you with Truth. You asked me what is the first thing I will do about "the problem" when I get home. I will bake a loaf of my incomparable bread and send it to Naomi. Then I shall buy the prettiest dress in town for Nani. As soon as I can manage it I shall go to Hawaii, where I will hold Nani, rock her, sing to her.

NO: She cannot hear!

I *(firmly):* I will sing to her. Do you know what I shall sing?

> Praise him,
> Praise him,
> All ye little children;
> God is love,
> God is love.

This really silenced No. Apparently the voices of No are completely routed by praise. It was a joyful discovery!

The closer I came to home, the more aware I became that my being, conscious and unconscious, was loosening its hold on the question of pain and suffering. It was as if its legs and arms relaxed and disengaged themselves mile after mile, until by the time I opened the door of home and was engaged by other arms, the grilling and probing and sifting and separating were stilled.

Much later that evening I read the accumulated mail, the letters from Naomi first.

One paragraph leaped out at me:

I have been happy these last months—full of joy. I mean full of joy. I wish I could paint "full of joy." It's beautiful! Yet it has been during my joy that my deepest, most honest grief has come. I feel both inside. There's no conflict. I think they build onto each other. It's strange!

Strange, yes! A mystery that the creature of the First Spontaneity, "the natural man," cannot understand without a profound change taking place deep within where the meanings are, and deeper still, where the spirit is. And it was happening! Yes, it *is* happening. And will go on happening.

"It looks as if our Naomi has found what you found on our river—the Catskill eagle," said my Partner.

"The Catskill eagle?"

Then my Partner took from the shelf his well-thumbed copy of Melville's *Moby Dick* and read:

There is a wisdom that is woe; but there is a woe that is madness. And there is a Catskill eagle in some souls that can alike dive down into the blackest gorges, and soar out of them again and become invisible in the sunny spaces. And even if he forever flies within the gorge, that gorge is in the mountains, so that even in his lowest swoop the mountain eagle is still higher than other birds upon the plain, even though they soar.

"It fits! It fits!" I cried in excitement. "It's in Isaiah!"

But they who wait for the Lord
shall renew their strength,
they shall mount up with wings
like eagles.

Afterword

When I wrote *Turn Over Any Stone,* I wrote as a victim experiencing not her first taste of suffering, but her first big taste of suffering. I was running away from my first overwhelming sense of the futility, the immensity, the helplessness of human suffering. The book was myself swinging around to confront the elements I did not wish to see, and in the process of writing the book I discovered more elements inside and outside me that I did not wish to see. But I discovered much more, and by the grace of God and the pondering that I recognize to be the work of the Holy Spirit, I am continually discovering more. Indeed, at times I almost cry out, "Will you leave me alone!"—but immediately postscript, "Please, please don't!"

It would be dishonest to pretend that in these twenty years there have been no more stones in Naomi's, Nani's, Partner's, and my lives (I shall continue to protect my daughter's and granddaughter's privacy by using fictitious names for them, although I will divulge that Nani's lovely Hawaiian name is Kamakia). Those massive boulders—divorce, alcohol, and drugs—have rolled into our lives as well, and not every one of us has turned them over to find Christ there. However, the promise and the possibility of that up-turning remains as constant as our love for one another.

Eleven years ago Naomi's marriage ended in divorce, and she returned home from Hawaii, where after the birth of two more children and because of Nani's need for full-time care, Naomi had to place her in an institution. Here at home Naomi attended and finished college and then found work to support her family. While she was a student, Naomi, my husband and I shared the care of her family but had to place Nani in a private, old, and well-established residence in our town for mentally retarded persons. She lives there still, two miles away from her grandparents and forty-five miles away from her mother's present home.

Nani is now twenty-two years old. She is five feet, five inches, tall and weighs eighty-five pounds. Her last annual medical examination diagnosed her as free of the psychomotor seizures she had as a child but as still suffering from mild thoraciolumbar scoliosis and mild planovalgus deformity. Her most recent professional psychological evaluation diagnosed her as profoundly retarded. The Stanford Binet Intelligence Scale estimated her IQ to be 24. The Vineland Social Maturity Scale test of her adaptive and developmental skills evaluated her social age as one year and two months.

So much for the professional evaluation! My afterword ends with Grandmother's Unprofessional, Undocumented Non-Test.

Nani Kamakia is beautiful. He skin is like fragrant cinnamon, her hair raven black, and her eyes like ripe olives. Twenty years ago she was thought to be deaf, but she hears normally with the ears of her body and her heart. She is nonverbal, but she speaks eloquently with eyes, face, and pleasant throat sounds. Like most mentally disabled persons, she enjoys eating but needs to have her food chopped and also requires assistance and supervision at meals. She walks, but, left unattended, wanders. She likes nothing better than to have someone she loves wander with her as she walks and wanders.

Nani Kamakia is very happy and therefore is very well liked by staff and peers at her home away from home. Her IQ may be lower than low, but her LQ (Love Quotient) is so high that it is immeasurable.

Every story has a beginning and an end. Some begin happily and end sadly. Some begin sadly and end happily. Be the ending happy or sad, the heart that loves will praise. Whatever the dark ways, whatever the twisted maze, the heart that loves will praise.

About the Author

Edna Hong collaborates with her husband in the translation of the works of Søren Kierkegaard. In 1968 the Hongs won the National Book Award for their translation of the first volume of Kierkegaard's *Journals and Papers*. Edna Hong has also collaborated with her husband in the production of eight children, who in turn have produced twenty grandchildren and three great grandchildren. Single-handedly, she has written and has published about a dozen books. The most recent titles are *Wild Blue Berries; Box 66, Sumac Lane;* and *Pulu Did It!*